inspired
girl
BOOKS

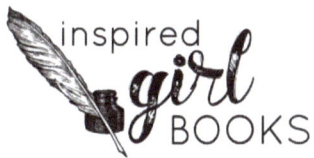

little miss
negative

Jennifer
Tuma-Young

Years ago, I wanted to begin a new venture.

Not with work (although that was part of it),

but with my whole life.

And there was this little voice
inside my head
that kept telling me:
"Just do it.
Take the darn leap,
and don't look back;
just spread your arms out
and believe that you will fly.
Believe that you will soar.
Believe that you are being
who you are meant to be.
Let your dreams be your wings,
and go for it."

But, then,

there was

this

other

voice.

The little voice that told me:
"Be practical.
Be realistic.
Your life is fine as it is now.
You don't need to make a
change. You've got
responsibilities.
You've got bills.
And no time.
You definitely don't have
time to change anything,
start something new,
chase a crazy dream.
You are an adult."

She had a point.
So I decided to take
the little voice,
the not-so-positive
little voice out dinner.

I thought I could
win her over
with my enthusiasm,
my tenacity,
my choice in fabulous
sushi hot spots.

I thought,
"Sure she thinks that now,
but wait 'til she hears
my plan.
She'll believe in me!"
We'll have a little chat,
me and that
little negative voice,
and she will come
to the other side.

This book is dedicated to anyone
who has ever entertained
the voice of self-doubt.

I got all dolled up
for our dinner.
I rehearsed my speech.
I couldn't wait
to convince her
that I was worth it.

But, after a nice
long meal,
she **still** stuck
her **tongue** out
at **me**.

She said excitedly:
"This was fun!
You're such an
understanding friend.
I put you down,
I squash your dreams,
and you
take me
to dinner!"

This was the only grin I got out of her the whole night.

So, that's when I decided to get the check and drop her off at the nearest bus station. I deleted that little negative voice from my phone, my iPad, my email, my head, and said my goodbyes.

It wasn't easy.
She had been a part
of my life for so long,
but it was time.
If I wanted
to move forward,
I had to break my ties
with the little
negative voice.

That same night, me and
the positive little voice
had a cup of tea,
and began creating
our vision!!
And we never
looked back.

About the Author

Jennifer Tuma-Young is the founder of Inspirista Lifestyle Design and creator of the Inspired Girl Blog. Over the past two decades, she has worked with thousands of women, and traveled the country speaking at events, for nonprofits, and in the media. Now, in her daily life, she is a proud momma of her two most precious gifts from God, and she is the co-creative force behind her family business, The Domesticated Dad Catering Company where she works with her incredible food-creating husband serving awesome, homemade meals in their community.

To connect with her online, sign up for the mailing list, download resources, and read the blog, visit http://inspiredgirl.net

www.ingramcontent.com/pod-product-compliance
Lightning Source LLC
Chambersburg PA
CBHW040941100426
42813CB00017B/2885